Precious Metals

Precious Metals

New and Selected Poems

Bill Lyons

PADDLE PRESS
NORTH LIBERTY, IOWA

Paddle Press, North Liberty, Iowa
Copyright © 2010 Bill Lyons
All rights reserved
Cover by Benjamin Chait, Chait Galleries Downtown, Iowa City, Iowa
Typeset by Sara T. Sauers, Iowa City
ISBN 13: 978-0-615-40434-9

for Caryl

Contents

New Poems

Winking at the Mouse

Yes, the house is so quiet
a writer can write this poem.

But she would need to be
as quiet as the mouse
under the Christmas tree
the mouse no one knows about
but me.

I know it's there because
we winked at each other.
It's that quiet.

Music

(to Caryl)

I thought I heard music this morning.
Turns out it must have been lingering notes
from that concert.
Of course the concert was good
because you were there
sitting in the stadium
with me
when you
might well have been
first clarinet in the
Music Under the Stars band.
The real music that evening was you, of course,
and this morning that must have been the music I heard.
I am the luckiest man.
I get to hear that music every day of my life.

Nested Tables

At their individual
stages of development.
Four legs each.

Sturdy
for coffee, tea, sodas
or exotic desserts.

"World Politics"
or "Sports Illustrated"
temporarily.

Catalogs,
children's books
and never-before drawings.

Wet sticky stuff
left
to harden.

Welcome
nested
tables.

Precious Metals

Our son plays guitar at open mikes
and wherever he can get on the program.
Tonight he plays at the Blue Peacock
or the Blue something. No matter the name
it won't be the same after Tim plays.
He has a golden touch on the strings,
adds silver when he sings.

Having a Plan

Flying west above a storm
I saw shards of light spark, crack.
I could not hear clouds rumble
thunder, roll east towards Ohio
but I wondered about children below
(say in "The Sound of Music")
running into the room of an adult
(maybe Julie Andrews') saying
oh I wanted to be sure you were all right
no I wasn't scared much but could I stay
with you for a while you know
so you won't be afraid.
Yes get under the covers. Thank you
for checking on me. Did you know
that fifty electrical storms are going on
at the same time around the world?
Thank goodness only one storm is here.
If all fifty storms come
dive under your pillow.

Shall We Dance?

Flying home from Alaska,
I looked at cumulus clouds
and   my floater
dancing

Dancing?
It followed my gaze
left   right   up
down

like a dance partner
following my lead
Out of the corner
of my eye

I observed
my vision jerking
here   there   anywhere
Concentrating

I slowed my floater
moved smoothly
around the dance floor
ended with a dip

To Flower

A businesswoman
hitting a glass ceiling

might remember
the yellow Larrea

of the Yukon
working its way

through ice.

Supper

Hopping toad
Hungry crows peck at his legs
Supper is served

Eye Exam

ophthalmologists ask   can you hold still
while I take a picture of your eye
she watches my right hand shake
until it rests   says STEADEEE

(shutter clicks too late)
then to her assistant   hold his head
forearms and hands tighten in a headlock
my whole body shaking now

it's my first "off" period
meds wearing off   symptoms up
she says to come back another day
just after taking my meds

Falling

weak legs aching uneven sidewalk
I hurry to catch up with my wife
and granddaughters one in a stroller
the other on a trike I stub my toe

as before I lead with head and glasses
taking the blow under my right eye
in the fleshy part of the high cheek
cut a two inch slit spilling blood

my wife doesn't want the girls to see
young as they are she hustles them
to her parents' home two blocks
brings our van takes me to the hospital

cat scan stitches black eye
ooh the girls say
they never saw the blood

Fireworks 2028

Twenty nations have announced
they will compete in the First
Nuclear-Missile Games.

Participants have agreed
to return fire on countries
that launch a missile.

Like boaters in harbor pulled in
to anchor and watch fireworks on land,
spectators board space capsules,

head out to dock at orbiting stations
and watch the nuclear explosions on Earth.
The winner? Last country standing.

There goes the first one!
"Ohhhhhhh. Ahhhhhhhh."

Parenting

I walked past the mother
to look more closely at the
child and the rope

tied around her waist
the other end tied
to a metal ring
hammered into the floor.

The rope was so short
she could not stand.
I asked the mother
"Why is the child tied?"

"We didn't want her
to hurt herself.
Ever since she was little,
whenever she tried to stand
she fell."

Suspended

Once in a hot air balloon
I felt suspended
because there was no wind.

Finally the pilot asked
if we preferred up
or down.

I realized
somebody in
Arizona or Rhode Island
China or Africa
was likely
also sitting
in the air
with no wind.

"Could we stay here a while?
Oh, and may I borrow your
binoculars?"

Territory

When we had apple trees
one branch came to a point

above the back steps. If we jumped
we could touch the robin's nest.

We knew not to touch the babies
or the nest, but the mother

seemed to worry that we might.
One time the robin's mate

swooped down at us the way
an owl swooped on the English river.

Two Girls

young maybe nine
hurried to the bookstore
not racing just eager
likely headed
for a favorite shelf of books
snuggling down into a soft chair

up again
hustling to other shelves
out into the mall walkway
on to the next and the next
leaving parents behind

such energy   eager to learn
moving with vigor and purpose
wanting not to miss anything
remarkable young girls
each with only one leg

Remembering

sometimes sometimes some freewriting
helps a person begin to write
something worthwhile something
that might turn into something by night

then again, again, again
sometimes it does not hot lot tot
at least one can get something
on paper

if a person gets bored she can write
something not boring like
the five-year-old
sat on the steps

remembering
when he was little

We're Home, Toto

When I awoke
I could not remember
which of our seven houses I was in.

When I put out my foot to go downstairs
I bumped into the fire fighters' pole.
I realized I was in our Florida home.
I remembered to grab the pole just in time.

The incident brought back memories
of the time in Montana when I reached
for the pole and fell down the stairs.
In Maine, in my sleepy condition, I stuffed
dirty clothes into the laundry chute
only to discover I had plugged the toilet.

In Texas, the house has no dishwasher.
I forgot and filled the refrigerator
with dirty dishes. I could go on.
You probably have had similar experiences
with your eleven houses.

Trauma at Age Two

She senses that Mama has left the room.
She checks the kitchen. Her brow furrows.

She hurries down the stairs. Her lip trembles.
 She climbs the stairs, runs to the couch,

scrambles up, puts her face to the window-glass,
cries, "Mama, my mama!".

She throws herself on the couch, sobbing,
"Mama! Mama. My mama. My *ma*ma."

Suddenly she looks toward the bedroom,
slides off the couch, runs the length of the hall,

drops to her hands and knees, looks under the bed.
She hears the front door open. "Mama?" she wails.

Dirty Clothes

Are they ready to be washed?
The pile of clothes in the wicker basket?
I no longer carry clothes to the stream.

Table Games

The seven-year-old says
let's play Monopoly
Uno Sorry chess Sequence
all at once if possible.

I'll win she says.
Winning is fun she says.
So she buys Boardwalk
reverses direction of play

switches pieces with an 11 card
checkmates with her queen
plays a ten of hearts
for a diagonal sequence

Let's play *again* she says.

Selected Poems

Two Views

I drift close to shore watching
turtles frogs raccoons fox deer flowers

looking at the shallows and behind
weeds two eyes ears nose quickly I

am past and new weeds obscure the view.

I stand close to shore watching
leaves twigs foam logs boats

looking at the water as it moves
drifting silver water quickly it

is gone I strain to see what has passed.

Choices

Now that a doctor has predicted
I may not live much longer,
I'll do things enjoyed, intended—
see the St. Louis Cardinals,

photograph Great Blue Herons,
read till I'm someone else,
fish for walleye in the Boundary
Waters of northern Minnesota.

Or, better, I'll sit people down,
look them in the eye, ask questions,
listen to their stories, nod, smile,
laugh, say tell it again and what

about that story you told yesterday
and last week and remember that one
you said was a favorite—when you
took the last piece of pie and your

sister chased you round and round
the house till you turned and threw
the pie in her face? Did she repay you?
Does she remember that story?

And what about the time your dad
killed the ringworm-cat with a hammer?
And when you leaned back against an open
flame on the stove, your shirt caught fire

and your mom put out the flames
with her bare hands? And vacations?
You said you slept on air mattresses
in parking lots—and traveled all over

the United States? And you and your brother
wrestled on the twin beds and how winning
meant pushing the other guy between the beds?
What other love stories do you have?

Cell Games

1. Johnny says he can run behind the foggers' jeep
longer than I can. As I run I think boy this DDT
will kill those mosquitoes. My mother tucks tissues
into the cracks around our windows. She says if this
stuff will kill insects it may harm people too
But she's my mom and I'm eleven and just starting
to say, well, *Johnny* is dancing with the fog.
Maybe I can be a Moses and part the stuff.

2. Flying above southern Illinois,
you can't see the poisons in the soil.
Ron and I ride on the back of a wagon.
Our legs dangle over.
Metal gleams in the summer sun.
Our hands grip the hoses that run to the tanks
filled for today with lead arsenate.

Louie drives the old, dirt-brown tractor,
the tenth year he has helped spray apple trees.
We grab the nozzles, aim
at the branches loaded with Jonathans,
and when Louie yells "Let 'em have it!"
we turn on the spray, anti-aircraft gunners
defending the country.
Ron's doing it, I'd have told my mom.
The liquid blows back in our faces.
We swear. We shoot more Jonathans. "Take that!"
Elsewhere the United States and the USSR
have settled into the Cold War.

At quitting time Louie tells us good job.
We look at each other, laugh,
"Let's do it again."

3. At Mayo's, Massachusetts General . . . .
bags of chemicals hang from IV poles. "Poison:
do not allow contents to touch your skin."
ARA-C, daunorubicin, and VP-116 course through your veins.
Let the healing begin

Haven't had infections in my mouth or anus before.
Diarrhea's my latest companion.
Vomiting? Even if I felt like eating . . . .
Doctors say we have to destroy the good fighter white cells
        to destroy the bad.

4. In Vancouver, a hepatitis C patient hopes for a cure.
In Boston it's a diabetic.
It's a sickle cell anemia patient in London
and an Alzheimer's victim in . . . I can't remember where.

Sitting in a Wooden Swing

on the wrap-
around porch,
low railing
a footstool,

blowing smoke rings
into fading light,
rings drifting touching,
two people talking,

crescent moon nestling
into the sunset beyond
railroad tracks where trains
carry coal to factories

to blow steam and smoke
but not like ours,
soft circles against
the coming stars.

A Fishing Eagle

The photograph I did not take shows an eagle
leaving its branch-woven nest high in a dead oak

on the far side of Mackenzie Lake, steering clear of my shore
flying to its right in what would become a counter-clockwise

tour of the lake, moving steady as the earth turning,
slow as the earth turning, in concert with the earth.

The photograph I did not take stops
time never to fade never to

change never to go to the next and the next
picture that counts moments of the eagle's

flight an oval path now lower now lower still
now angling toward the water slowly surely

as though the route had been envisioned from
the nest, pictured silently carried out silently

my ears straining for the gentle powerful whoosh
of wings moving air, but hearing only my heart

pulsing. Then, talons aimed, the eagle touches
down, tear of claws through scales, now up

moving toward its nest, away from me
a rubber raft angled over my head to block the rain.

Early Morning Quiet

When Bill Knowles delivered the
   St. Louis Globe-Democrat
   and I delivered the
   Chicago Daily-News
we'd meet at Sycamore and Almond
   at five o'clock, before light,
   and slide on the ice on our bikes
   trying not to lose any newspapers
   or, worse, have the paperbag
   come off the handlebars,
   automatic victory for the other guy.

The streets were ours then
   and where our routes overlapped
   and some customers took
   both our papers
we'd throw together, trying to
   hit the porch and
   slide the paper to the door,
   without hitting the glass milk bottles,
   like a horseshoe sliding to the stake.

Snow made it even quieter,
   bike tracks illuminated
   by streetlights and
   porch lights dimmed
   by soft snow.

Now, thirty-five years later,
   early morning quiet
   reminds me of those days. My wife and I slip
      the canoe

into the Wapsipinicon River at Waubeek
   and drift south towards Stone City.

It is just light, and a
   great blue heron lifts himself
   into the river's dawn
   to guide us on our way.

The sun hits the treetops
   as we approach the first turn,
   paddles dipping silently,
   guiding the bow into the longest V.

Once through and into quiet water again,
   Caryl and I look back, and smile,
   and see ripples. Or is it—bike tracks
   illuminated by streetlights?

A Walk Near Water

When the evening comes, and it will come,
to walk near water one last time,
I'd like to take that walk with you,
hand in hand along a shore
of lake or river we've canoed.

We need not be there in the flesh,
hats, shoes, long pants and sleeves,
as long as in our hearts we know
the oneness that so strengthens us
each time we touch and say hello.

We've paddled together all these years,
on quiet water, white water, white caps.
A walk near water might well be,
if lake or river we've canoed,
our version of eternity.

Being Heard

I lie awake
remembering my mother
canoeing one week,
facing death the next.

Nitroglycerine patches
ease her pain,
slow the pulse.

Mom speaks, but
I don't understand her.
I hold her oxygen mask.

She moves her lips a second time
(without her dentures I realize now),
I smile, say, "Please say that again.
My hearing's not what it used to be."

I bend over till I feel her breath
on my ear. I smile at her. She smiles, too.
I place the oxygen mask
back over her face.

She closes her eyes,
having said
what she wanted to say.

Celebration of Morning

at sunrise flute music floats across square lake
loons cock their heads peer though mist

then answer, their trills matching the flute
notes wafting back and forth back and forth

riding on mist poking through mist
alerting the boundary waters to a new sound

the man sets down his flute picks up his coffee cup
leans against a rock watches the loons swim closer

a chickadee offers its call, tentatively, aware of the
keen competition the sonorous sounds echoing

one a celebration of morning the
other an answer welcome greeting

the chickadee comes other chickadees a
gull sailing on wind currents cries eeeee

dives as though to join the musicians warming
but instead to snare a fish and climb up and fly

to other lakes songs musics back and forth
these new notes introducing the day

*(In honor of David Evans' flute playing
on the Kawishiwi/Square Lake Boundary
Waters Canoe Area trip, summer of 1999)*

Union Station, St. Louis, 1964

I help my mother up the steps
to the passenger train, whites
in the left car, blacks in the right car,
on their own.

At the top of the steps, I turn right,
not looking to see if she is following.
She slows but moves towards me.
The people in the car stop talking.

I show her to a seat, give her a hug,
tell her to have a good trip home.
She smiles at me, a smile I have
never seen, a smile that says
oh bill please don't.

Luggage Rack Lullaby
(for Mildred)

You say the wind whistling
through the luggage rack went away
when the two parts were pushed together
like twins made to wear matching outfits
or adults on a blind date.

Perhaps it's in my closet
in a box that used to hold milkweed pods
until that Saturday in spring
when I opened the box to the sky
and let the wind caress the pods
until they rose into the air
soft and light as butterflies.

Or maybe the wind has gone
to find another luggage rack,
one that is spread out,
one that will let the wind whistle
when the car goes between—
what did you think? 35 and 40
miles per hour? You say it's more
fun to drive now that the wind is gone?

I don't know. The wind doesn't visit
just anyone. I think it picked you special,
as a driver who would let it sing.
If it were me, I'd loosen that rack a little,
just enough to let the wind visit now and again.
Some people live their whole lives
and never hear the wind.

Mary

will buy an old-fashioned
motorless lawn mower
if they have one
in the warehouse.

The computer lists 10
in aisle 5, but there are none
in aisle 5 or aisles 4 or 6.

The man driving the forklift cruises
all the aisles, looking for push mowers.
As his Frustration Mounts, he Accelerates

AND ZOOMS DOWN AISLE 5
ONE LAST TIME, YELLING
"PUSH MOWERS, COME OUT!"

But the push mowers are hiding behind
8 boxes of gas grills and 14 boxes of hose winders.
So Mary buys the floor model.

Mr. Sullivan

Wide-eyed cats arch, hiss.
Four white, black-ticked English

setters, forty pounders, penned
since last night, pump leg muscles,

lift paws, watch the gate,
wag tails, hear the latch click,

explode through neighbors'
justblooming tulips, daffodils,

thunder past Mr. Sullivan,
out for his evening stroll.

Ownership

In the fifties, the colored man (Mike's dad called him)
daily urged his old horse down the rutted alley
spotted with potholes, manure, and dried food scraps.
Garbage cans he dumped into the front half of the wagon,
leaning, with cracked rotting boards and bald rubber tires.

The pile of furnace ashes he shoveled into the back half,
taking the whole pile until all that remained was level ground.
In a way the alley belonged to the colored man.
Once Mike burned trash on a windy day. Flames reached the
neighbor's pine tree. The next day the colored man looked

at the blackened trunk and branches where before had been
green needles of the white pine, brown pine cones and bark.
"How'd that happen? You do that?" From that day on,
the colored man, the neighbor, even Mike's family knew,
in a way, the blackened trunk and branches belonged to Mike.

Skunk River Blues

South of Delta the Skunk makes a hypotenuse between
highways 92 and 21 we asked the deputy at the Delta parade

65 tractors any logjams no we put in under high-up
overhanging branches streaks of light coming through

from the south then after about the fifth bend a logjam
lay stretched ahead and to the right one hundred yards long

logsmudoldappliancescarspartsoffarmbuildingsmorelogs

we walked around the jam mud three feet deep from water
at flood stage just days before even the cornfields soaked

from floodwaters carried canoe ice chest paddles life vests
back to the water we rinsed our clothes free of mud paddled

down river to the car pulled the canoe up water-soaked banks
covering ourselves with mud again loaded canoe cartop tied down

mud dripped from the canoe onto the windshield hood trunk
rough looking character drove down our lane seed cap

sleeveless shirt rusty rattly pickup dented front end he said
you're not hunters no we laughed then we saw the back of his

sign up the lane later at the general store 12-year-old girls
talked quietly giggled pointed at us obviously blue with envy

Aesthetic Distance

Canoeing the Wapsipinicon
we listen to the dipping of our paddles
the lapping of water on the hull.

Around a bend, vultures
wrinkled-orange faces
watch us approach.

They fly. Later we see them
rising on thermals
soaring on motionless wings.

Kid Memories

we moved when I was 11 suddenly I was
the fastest runner except for sherry tallest
smartest along with petey payne I got a paper route
the chicago daily news rode my bike all over
no hands judy goddard and I and her younger
sister met at the rogers theater each saturday
10 cents sat together walked to her house then
I walked home to my dogs chipper and zipper
we'd sit on the doghouse roof talk enjoy the day

touch football was big in our narrow backyard
until carl bateman ran hard around right end
stiff-armed bill wallace ran into the steel
clothesline post we played baseball on the lot
between the martin's and the bateman's broke
a window at each house but kept playing
once I gave a halfback fake to harry wallace
chasing me but I couldn't escape so I hopped
on my bike wiggled the front wheel to fool him
catapulted over the handlebars broke my elbow
went on collecting for the daily news till a
fraternity guy I woke up to collect from said
hey kid you're crying are you hurt then I called
my mom and we went to the hospital

an X on our front sidewalk probably was put
there my mother said by a hobo who had gotten
a handout this was 1949 marking our house

I walked with granddad past the
piggley wiggley to mcbride's drug
lemon meringue pie at the counter

granddad tripped and fell as we walked
lay on the sidewalk looked up at me
said now billy when you fall the key is
to relax that's how not to break anything
grandma helped me with a card table
sidewalk store cigar box with change
behind the counter bunting gum candy
lifesavers little paper american flags

johnny marshall and I rigged a mail
system between the second story porch
and the cherry tree club house a long
string making a continuous loop
attached messages to the top string
pulled the bottom string

johnny and I swam in the horse trough from
the attic crawled through old furnace pipes
in the yard hung on a rope went hand over
hand from the peak of the garage where
someone had written "kilroy was here" to the
cherry tree lit my brother's tissue
stick-model plane for life-like air battles
afterwards we tried to blow out the flames

in the winter I leaned a leaf from the dining room
table against the bottom rung of a chair raced
marbles down the board out onto the rug marbles
that went farthest won each color a big ten
team illinois orange michigan blue ohio state red

marbles also could be rolled on the front porch
sloped to the rotted-out low corner where a hole
waited I had to guard against marbles going

through the hole and under the porch spider webs
old jars bricks dirt piles made by who knew what
animals at the back of the house the stucco slabs had
broken away under the lilac bushes access to mystery
marble tournaments were the thing at leal the urbana
schools had city wide tournaments I had steelies
glassies shooters john bell could knock two marbles
out of the ring with one shot I won once

after an illinois-ohio state football game
I danced like chief illiniwick headdress
flying knees lifted high bow in one hand
bare spot in the front yard grass

one evening I put on my cowboy boots hat
holster cap pistol ran out of the house in
search of a bad guy I think ran smack into
a big man walking towards me he caught
me I said sorry ran on down the sidewalk
shooting my cap pistol every which way

I helped kit bannister with his morning paper
route saturday or sunday was his day to sleep in
kids rode by on tricycles ringing their bells kit
shot his b-b-gun at them to make them go away

I rode the city bus to visit my dad at his
office I got directions at the standard oil
station from a man who knew my dad

at leal I was called little lump because when
my brother jim went there he was called lump
walking home from leal I don't know why
I swore at passing drivers hid behind

small trees my skinny body sticking out on both
sides one driver stopped yelled at my tree
in winter I threw snowballs at cars a driver told
me I could break a windshield hurt someone

I told another student I didn't like the teacher
when the teacher asked why I didn't like her
I said I liked her and I didn't know why
I told the student what I did I still don't know

my older brother slid down a tree next to the
second story porch that opened off our bedroom
he'd go on dates meet the guys shinny up
the tree later tiptoe into our room one night
I saw a shadow on the porch did not know he was
gone ran to mom in the next bedroom dad in
the backyard with the double barreled shotgun
I might have fired dad said I thought dad why
weren't you inside the shadow came inside

two university students roomed at our house
they had big motorcycles had been stationed
on submarines during the war now I know
they were going to school on the GI bill
my dad was a reporter for the champaign
news-gazette some nights he was a watchman at
city park he carried a billy club but no gun

once I opened the bathroom door not knowing
my grandmother was in her birthday suit
her hair down to the floor I stood and watched

Mental Acuity Tests

neurologists ask   who is president?
day and date?   spell world backwards?
study for the test? d-l-r-o-w d l r o w
studying makes the test inaccurate

but so what meds only moderate symptoms
people with failing memories (I've heard)
remember language longer if it comes within a song
I can imagine a neurologist asking me

to sing a song I know by heart
"My home town is a one horse town
but it's good enough for me,
doop doop, *doop* doop, *doop*-pa-doop, *doop* . . . "

and the neurologist thinks with a smile, "Ah ha!
Can't remember words even in a favorite song."
and I'll get to say, "Those *are* the words
my family always sings."

Early Morning Intimacy

He touches her,
holds her close,
more than when
he was a macho man.

Now when they
awaken during the night
they touch hands,
squeeze, stroke, caress.

When the
clock radio plays,
she smiles, comes around
the bed, lifts the
covers a little, rubs
still-swollen feet.

Handclap Fingersnap

When three-year-old Tim
dances, chairs sit up,
plates rattle in rhythm,
tumblers tap their toes,

the dining room rocks to and fro
with a handclap fingersnap,
knee-bend swing-dip. The house
shimmies, struts off its foundation

into the street. Other houses sway,
strain, strut, break away, join in.
Trees clap their branches. Leaves
wave in syncopated measures.

Hydrants bend to the beat,
shoot streams of water
higher than the houses
as the music man dances on.

Angling for Smiles

Canoeing on the inlet stream
we come upon two boys fishing.

Seeing us, the younger one
scrambles from his seat
under the old railroad bridge,

slips down the mud bank,
holds up a stringer.
A six-pound catfish.

Hmmm

is what my wife says sometimes.
That's all she says. "Hmmm."

In the back of her mind she
must know I'm there in the room
waiting for more information.

But the "hmmm" stands alone
whenever I can bear to let it.

Time

The American Heritage Dictionary
  ticktock ticktock

defines *time* as: a nonspatial continuum
  before people

in which events occur in apparently irreversible
  sun moon tides

succession
  august september

from the past through the present
  thickness of a rabbit's coat

to the future
  baby youth adult aged
  illness death remembered
    forgotten

Snow Day

A free day. That's what a snow day is.
Herbert Hoover said days spent fishing
do not count against you.
A snow day is like that. It's for music,

poetry, long telephone conversations
writing, reading, and yes, shoveling snow.
But on the right kind of snow day, there's no point
shoveling 'cause the wind's not through blowing.

It's for doing anything you couldn't justify on a work day.
And students (and teachers) are so happy.
Not snow plowers, parents of unsupervised children,
baby-sitters taking extra shifts.

For some, it's a day for dreaming, of, say, canoeing:
reserving a put-in spot for the Boundary Waters,
hitting the water loaded to the gunnels,
paddles dipping and swinging, swirls in the water,

a heron rising from the shallows, loons turning their heads
sharply in the middle of the lake, giving a single call,
a beaver swimming around the point so quietly,
now the bow of the canoe slicing through gentle waves.

On Three

It was the man fallen to cold ground
that focused the late afternoon
against patchy snow,
the pin oak almost barren of leaves,
the daughter giving CPR,
faint sirens, cars parked wherever.
Lights bounced off houses,
neighbors converged
from cooking a roast,
watching Oprah,
"Googling" the internet for articles on ALS,
scheduling a United flight to Boston.
Paramedics alternated compressions, ventilations,
the daughter pleaded with them to save her dad,
pleaded with her dad to live.
Electric shock paddles on three

Driving in Scotland

I focus on the narrow road's "wrong side."
Rock walls lurk close to the shoulders.
Trucks hog the center line, honk.
Farm wagons drop hay on my windshield.

A red sports car careens up behind,
zooms around on a hill,
black car suddenly close to my bumper.

The clockwise roundabout, scene
of my counter-clockwise blunder, trucker
blocking traffic for my three-point turn.
"Americans!" drivers likely muttered.

The passengers in my car talked about sheep
grazing peacefully on the rolling hills.
I didn't see them. But we didn't crash.

Frosty Morning

I choose for my late-autumn stroll
a zigzag trail to Lookout Knoll.
It's not a walk up Rockies bold,
peaks dressed up, white shawls for cold.

Atop my knoll, the view I see
of red oak leaves, of gold and green
a patchwork makes, a splendid scene.
Let mountains dress while leaves preen.

Wind helps leaves let go their grasp
'cept pin oak leaves; they face the blast
of late fall rain and sleet at last,
storms like those ". . . Before the Mast."

I think of people on other knolls
around the world, watching scenes,
late-autumn nature. With me, they ask:
"Whose world is this?" I think I know.

Hypothetically

(for Nina)

Say
a person spilled most
of a jug of pineapple juice
on the kitchen floor.

And say
he has mopped it
wet and dry
for about 20 minutes.

What else
should he do?

Silver Flash

In the hammock, shaded by pine and aspen,
Lander, Wyoming newspaper
covering my face from the sun,
Thoreau's *Walden* within arm's length.
A trout leaps, twists,
catches a dragonfly, slaps the water.
My daughter brings our fishing rods.
I pretend sleep but she pokes me.
Smiling beneath my paper, I
grumble about how to carry
all the trout we will catch. She says
she will help carry the big ones.
We will be Hemingway and friend.
On the far side of the lake
a moose lumbers in the shallows.
We walk toward the trout hot spots.
"There's a deer," she says. "Beautiful."
We go on, fish for trout, love
 being outdoors as much as fishing.
When we do catch a fish, she says,
"You're not keeping that trout, are you?"
Well, I'm Hemingway, after all.
We look up. The moose is watching.
"On second thought," I say, "maybe
we should throw him back."
Silver flash.

The Path
(after Billy Collins)

You know the gravel road that turns left
after you cross the river on highway 965?
That road goes west a little ways,
then forks north to Swisher and straight
to the Hawkeye Wildlife Area. And
you know that first parking area on the right,
next to the woods? Squirrels leap in the treetops,
bending branches, flagging their location.

Just inside the woods line, a path starts left,
up the hill, parallel to the river, just wide enough
for one person. After while you come to a fallen tree
blocking your way. People have worn a new path
around it. The sun is in the southwest.
Before long you come to a lookout
at the top of the cliff. The view south
is at least a half mile across the Iowa River.

The best time to go is October,
when the leaves are gold and red,
in late afternoon, when the wind is still
and the sky is deep blue and cloudless.
If you're quiet, you can hear squirrels
cutting walnuts, hickory nuts, and acorns.
Perhaps some time I'll see you there.

Department of Anatomy

That's the answer to my granddaughter's question
"Where will you go when you die, Granddad?"
I like that answer a lot. It's true in the sense that
she can check it out. It doesn't depend on faith.

There is one possible glitch, though. At the top of the
Medical History form is this statement: "Falsification
of this document could lead to rejection at time of death."
Ah! As if rejection during life weren't enough.

I have a wonderful collection of rejection letters
from journals that publish poetry: The New Yorker,
The Iowa Review, The Paris Review (to name a few).
One can joke about being turned down by editors.

But rejected by a Department of Anatomy? Not fair.
I wouldn't be there to defend myself, to make fun, to respond.
Think what they'd be missing! My wife—the great hypothesizer—
is always wondering if one thing might have led to another.

Doesn't hurt to wonder, I suppose. Maybe when the
anatomy students cut me open to probe and poke and do all
manner of exploring they could actually find answers that
would help someone. I can hear the discussion.

"See this odd cell under high power where it says
'1952, ran back and forth through DDT clouds from
mosquito-foggers'?" "Look at this: Five strangely
shaped cells under a sign: '1957, sprayed apple trees

(and himself) with lead arsenate'." If my granddaughter asks,
"Why the Department of Anatomy, Granddad?"
I'll say, "Well, ail those years I helped students learn.
This lets me help them learn a little longer."

Dangerous Liaisons

Waves crash
against rocks.

Lightning flashes,
crackles.

Sparks dance
on our metal canoe.

We paddle harder.

Funeral Visitation

I'm telling you, that hot-water chocolate cake
is the most moist cake I have ever tasted.

Well, that mayonnaise chocolate cake Martha
made is awfully moist, too. But not like the

hot-water cake, no sir. You're right,
the hot-water cake is *the* moistest cake.

What about the whipped-cream chocolate cake
Gertrude made for the summer city-wide potluck?

Yeah, that was good. That was moist, too But not
like the hot-water cake. Now THAT was moist.

Ghosts of Grief

Ghosts of grief visit now and then.
usually at a time of their choosing.
Dickens might have called them ghosts
of grief in the past, present, and future.

People die and the rest of us go on living.
Frost said it when the boy sawed off his hand.
Brueghel painted it when Icarus flew too near
the sun, melted the wax on his feathers, drowned

while others went about their business.
Ghosts of Grief Past remind us of losses—
relatives, friends, pets, hearing, lovers,
those lost through war, crime, disease.

Ghosts of Grief Present challenge us to thrive
even as we fade into relics of the past.
"Rage! Rage! against the dying of the light,"
but even Dylan Thomas returned to dust.

Perhaps we are most intrigued by Ghosts
of Grief Future and the possibilities they hold.
We know them only as apparitions—
butterflies and hummingbirds, flying.

Mountain Road

blasted out of rock,
cliffs straight up and down,
sometimes no guardrail
to bump you back onto the road.

I am driving on the outside
when a recreational vehicle
drifts over the centerline.
I squeeze towards the edge.

We pass. I sweat, shake, stiffen,
stop the car on the centerline,
walk to the inside wall.
"Somebody else drive."

I sit on the passenger side,
grip the door pull,
watch the inside rock wall,
picture sitting in a meadow.

I may not be afraid of dying,
but on this road,
I am afraid of falling.

Ode to a Lightweight Canoe

O, lightweight canoe,
friend to old men
who can still lift you,
though not your heavy brothers,
rock-bangers for swift rivers.

I can load you onto the car,
slip silently into quiet water,
paddle through reflected clouds,
drift in breezes soft as a mother's breath
    on her baby's cheek,
dip and swing in wind, whitecapped waves,
cut at an angle, slash head on,
    through rollers two feel high, water drenching us,
    then in wind stiff but congenial,
sail, paddles pointed skyward,
    lashed to thwarts,
    poncho tied between,
    finally,
drift again, with gentle breezes on my skin.

O, lightweight canoe,
when a portage looms,
time to carry you to the next lake,
I can swing you from the ground up to my shoulders,
bounce you for balance,
my hands lightly grasping the gunwales,
ready to throw you clear, if I fall,
ready to secure my balance if the trail
    turns rocky, mossy, marshy.

I stride along, jewelweed in patches
	with its orange, hanging blossoms
	in among red and blue cardinal flowers,
	black-eyed Susans,
	wild bergamot and tiger lilies
	all on a carpet of wild blueberries.
Now and again I pause—
	with you, my lightweight canoe,
	still resting on my shoulders—
	to pick raspberries,
	listen to the CAW CAW of a crow,
	the EEE of a gull.

Soon I see the lake
through evergreen needles and aspen leaves,
sunshine waltzing on whitecaps as they crest and fall.
We'll be there soon, lightweight canoe.
I hear a beaver slap its tail.
I hear a loon call, its voice a tremolo.

Learning Poems by Heart

Across the street on the wrap-around
porch, the Robert Frost group is meeting.

Now and then I hear a line and in my reverie
put line and line together in new form.

"I am one acquainted with the night"
"no more so than became a man"

"it was a risk I had to take—and took"
"this saying good-by on the edge of the dark"

Yestreen Night

At 19, Dusban supported nine siblings
smuggling guns, drugs, and people
across the Adriatic Sea, in the black of night
Albania to Italy

When Italian patrols spotted his speedboat
they pursued, engines whining.
Dusban dumped his cargo, roared away
to avoid capture, imprisonment or death.

Some people he threw overboard had life vests.
Sometimes those who did not could swim.
Searchlights, sharks, jagged rocks, undertow
hum of speedboats, cries of people in the water

Revival Meeting

The congregation was singing
"This little light of mine
I'm gonna let it shine . . ." Softer now.
"All ye who are weary and heavy laden
think tonight about confessing your sins
about asking God for forgiveness
about letting your light shine for Jeezus."

Kenny leaned forward
touched Judy's bra.

"I know you're in this congregation tonight
listening for the invitation to be born again
through Jeezus Christ Our Lord. Each of you
who wishes to dedicate your life to Jeezus
come forward while we sing."

Now Kenny tried to unsnap Judy's bra
through her blouse.
She turned around and frowned.

"Softly and tenderly Jesus is calling
calling for you and for me . . .
Come forward now as the spirit of God
moves you, kneel here by the bales of straw
and dedicate your life to Jeezus."

Kenny pulled the bottom of Judy's blouse
out away from her back
quickly ran his other hand up her bare skin
unhooked her bra. She whirled and glared at us.
The minister was watching.
Maybe if I did what Kenny was doing

I could get in trouble too and not have to
lead vespers for the other boys in my tent
after the service.

"Softly and tenderly Jesus is calling . . . .
A minister will pray with you and talk
with you as long as you want."

As long as I want?
My little light glowed like a bulb
above my head.

I went forward, knelt beside the straw.
Reverend Kean greeted me.
"God bless you, son. I'll pray with you."
"Th-th-thank you, Reverend K-K-K-Kean."

I asked God to forgive me for
throwing my sister out the back door
breaking her collarbone
accidentally burning down
the neighbor's evergreen tree
masturbating
tearing shingles off the garage roof
sailing them across the back yard
missing a block in football
Donnie getting helmet-spear-tackled
in his kidney
squirrel hunting on private property
racing in my folks' car
cheating on a test
hitting my mother
ringing doorbells, running

kicking Sheila's glass of ice tea
after my first kiss

Other kids came forward
to kneel and pray.
Finally someone announced
vespers were canceled.

Tuning Up

A black hole speaks
in a B-flat tone
57 octaves
below middle C.

Natasha practiced clarinet
in the neighbors' barn loft
while she watched the stars.
Once she didn't come home.

All-State Band
had trombones, flutes,
even bells and a piccolo,
but no B-flat clarinets.

Walking Above Iowa City

(after Billy Collins' "Walking Across the Atlantic")

I wait until no one is watching
before stepping barefoot onto a current of air.

Soon I am walking above Iowa City,
looking down at City Park,
watching for hot air balloons.

I feel air currents shifting under my feet.
Tonight I will sleep above Kinnick Stadium.

What will people think of me at tomorrow's game,
walking high above the line of scrimmage,
the calluses on my feet visible for the first time?

To Caryl—Caregiver

Your being a caregiver when I had leukemia
helped me to live. Now you have taken on
the caregiver role again, this time for a

Parkinson's patient. I have a special interest
in your willingness to serve in this role, your
generosity of spirit, since I am the patient again.

Is this what the minister meant when he said
"for better or for worse, till death do us part"?
I know I'm still in the "honeymoon" period

in terms of Parkinson's symptoms: tremor,
fatigue, cramped handwriting, slow movement
including slow eating, and unsteady balance.

But as I anticipate additional symptoms
over the years, my courage is strengthened
by your presence, your humor, your love.

Thanks for taking on the caregiver role, Caryl.
May your courage, and your energy,
be strengthened by my love for you.

BILL LYONS taught secondary English in a suburb of St. Louis, Missouri and in Iowa City, Iowa. Also, he taught in the Iowa Writing Project. His poems have appeared in *Aura Literary Arts Review*, *California Quarterly*, *The Christian Science Monitor*, *The English Journal*, *Lyrical Iowa*, *Rockford Review*, *360 Degrees*, *Xavier Review*, and elsewhere.

ALSO BY BILL LYONS
The Air Between Eyes, Quietwater, Trails and Campfires, Meshing Theory and Practice in the Teaching of Writing, Canoe Stories, On Three. Pieces in *Living with Parkinson's Disease*, edited by David Belgum. A variety of chapters, articles, and reviews related to the teaching of English.

Acknowledgments

Aura Literary Arts Review
    "Early Morning Intimacy"
    "Sitting in a Wooden Swing"
    "Union Station, St. Louis, 1964"
The Briar Cliff Review
    "A Fishing Eagle"
California Quarterly
    "Ownership"
The Christian Science Monitor
    "Two Views"
Cider Press Review
    "Choices"
The English Journal
    "Early Morning Quiet"
Hidden Oak
    "A Walk Near Water"
Iconoclast
    "Cell Games"
Living with Parkinson's Disease
    "To Caryl—Caregiver"
    "Mental Acuity Tests"
Lyrical Iowa
    "A Celebration of Morning"
Paper Street
    "Angling for Smiles"
Pennsylvania English
    "Skunk River Blues"
The Rockford Review
    "Handclap Fingersnap"
    "Flutterdance Bang"
    "Mary"
    "Luggage Rack Lullaby"
    "Being Heard"

Small Brushes
    "Aesthetic Distance"
    "Mr. Sullivan"
360 Degrees
    "Mental Acuity Tests"
Xavier Review
    "Hmmm"

Made in the USA
Charleston, SC
08 October 2013